This book belongs to: _____

To those who have loved deeply and lost greatly ~ this book is for you.

May you always feel the warmth of their love in the sunshine, hear their laughter in the wind, and find their hugs in the arms of those still here.

Inspired by our sweet daughter:
Caitlyn Alaska Hirschi Wilson

Copyright © Kristine Anne Hirschi, 2025. All rights reserved. No part of this book may be reproduced or transmitted in any form without permission, in writing, from the author.

ISBN: 979-8-9931638-3-3
Imprint: Independently published

Cover design and artwork by Allie Turek
Families Are Forever artwork by
Hazel Staples @hazel_paints
Printed in the United States of America

Grandma, where are you?
I've looked all around.
Grandma, where are you?
You cannot be found.

I've looked in the kitchen,
where we like to bake.

I thought maybe you would be baking a cake.

I've looked in the spaces
that you love to be.
I'm looking for you,
are you looking for me?

We always play games before I have a nap. We even read books as I sit on your lap.

People say you're in Heaven. But where is that place?

―――――――

If I knew
how to find
it, I'd hurry.
I'd race.

―――――――

I'd race to your bedside to get me a hug.
To snuggle and squeeze you, to feel of your love.

No, I cannot find it.
It's not on a map.

But I see you in dreams when I'm taking my nap.

*My sweet little child,
Heaven truly is real.
It's a place and a space
that for now you must
feel.*

It's here and it's there. It is everywhere! A place of pure joy, without any care.

*I know you can't see me
so trust when I say,
I'm with you sweet child,
every day.*

*With Heaven so close, can you feel that I'm near?
I'm cheering you on. If you listen, you'll hear.*

*You'll hear me in windchimes.
You'll feel me in hugs.
All the beauty around you?
That's me giving loves.*

A flower that's wild with colors so bright.
When you see them, you'll feel just a bit of my light.

*A butterfly's visit should brighten your day.
When you see it, you'll know that I've come your way.*

*In a sunset with colors
as bright as can be.
That is me smiling down,
I wish you could see.*

―――――――

*I'm near you.
I know you.
I love you so much.
Even though I'm away and you can't feel my touch.*

―――――――

*For I am in Heaven,
a place you can't see.
But my spirit is with
you for eternity.*

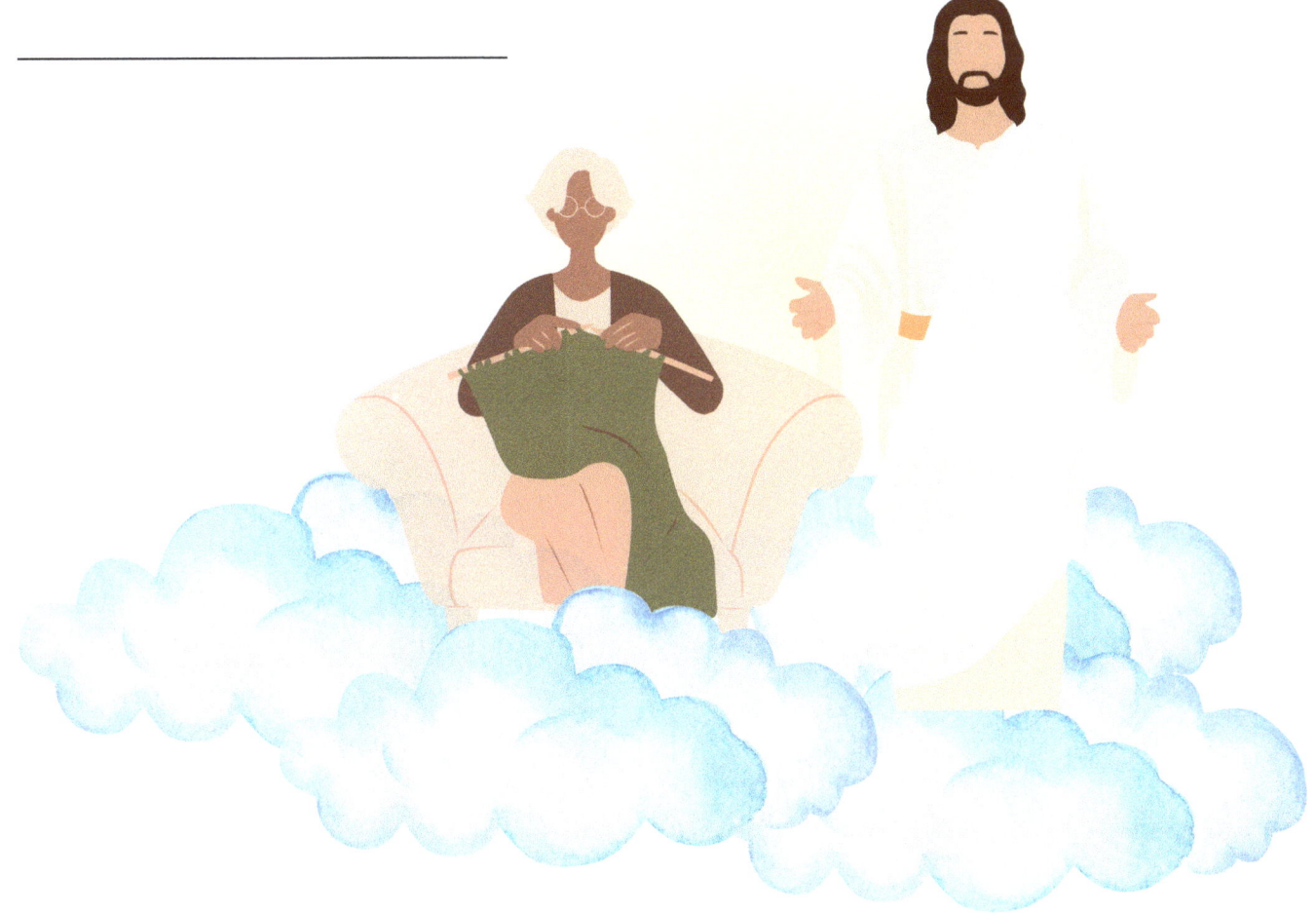

Then one day I'll see you and hold you so close.

But for now you must trust that ...

I love you the most!

Love,

Grandma

Families are forever

About the Author:

Kristine Hirschi resides in Hurricane, Utah with her husband, Michael. She is the mother of 8 wonderful children and is "Grammy Shirshi" to 14 grand-children - at the time of this print. Kristine loves writing and recently published a collection of 8 books written in poetry form. She is at the beginning of a promising literary career with many more children's publications ahead.

Grandma, Where Are You? is an endearing and comforting children's book. You can enjoy Kristine's other books in this collection by purchasing:

Mommy, *Where Are You?*
Daddy, Where Are You?
Grandpa, Where Are You?
Brother, Where Are You?
Sister, Where Are You?
My Friend, Where Are You? and
My Child, Where Are You?

Each book is written to give children, and adults alike, a sense of peace at the passing of a loved one.

To my dear readers ~

I want to share a portion of my heart with you and tell you how this book (and the entire Where Are You?) collection came to be. You see, in December of 2022 our third daughter, Caitlyn, was due to deliver her second son. Because of severe complications she passed away just 9 days after delivering her perfect baby boy. She left behind her 16-month old son and her 9-day old baby boy along with her husband and countless family and friends who still grieve her loss to this very day. Her husband has married an angel woman who is diligently determined to make sure all of their children know and love Mommy Caitlyn. She is a blessing to us all.

When Caitlyn's oldest son was 3, he came, with his family to visit Papa and Grammy Shirshi. Upon entering the house, he saw a picture of "Mommy Caitlyn". With his big, contagious smile, he turned to me and said, "Grammy! It's Mommy Caitlyn!!"
"Yes, sweetheart, it's a picture of Mommy Cait", I replied, with a lump in my throat and tear filled eyes. He immediately turned to his daddy and yelled with excitement, "Daddy, Maybe she's here!"
He then began running through my house, room to room, yelling "Mommy, Where Are You!?"

With broken hearts we sobbed as we tried to find the words to tell him that mommy's spirit was here but that he couldn't see her. We struggled to make sense of telling a young child "where" Heaven was, how he could feel her spirit in the beauty around him and even feel her presence.

This moment in time weighed heavily on my heart until in the early hours of a crisp November morning when I was awoken from a deep sleep with the words to a powerful poem pounding my mind. I rose immediately and began writing. When I was finished, the Mommy, Where Are You? poem was born and, from that, this book came to be. In the days that followed, I could not help but feel like these books needed to be shared with others who may be going through a similar situation in their lives.

If you are one of these people, I want to offer my deepest condolences to you, your family and your loved ones. My heart knows yours and I mourn with you in your time of great loss. May Heaven smile down upon you and bring comfort and peace to your soul.

~Kristine Hirschi

www.ingramcontent.com/pod-product-compliance
Lightning Source LLC
Chambersburg PA
CBHW051326110526
44582CB00003B/65